Prayer you will be blessed as you read

Carol

Psalm 139

He Giveth More
GRACE

a memoir

Carol I Vogt

 FriesenPress

Suite 300 - 990 Fort St
Victoria, BC, V8V 3K2
Canada

www.friesenpress.com

Copyright © 2017 by Carol I Vogt
First Edition — 2017

Scripture taken from the Holy Bible, NEW INTERNATIONAL VERSION®.
Copyright © 1973, 1978, 1984, 2011 by Biblica, Inc. All rights reserved worldwide.
Used by permission. NEW INTERNATIONAL VERSION® and NIV® are
registered trademarks of Biblica, Inc. Use of either trademark for the offering of
goods or services requires the prior written consent of Biblica US, Inc. Scripture
quotations taken from the Amplified® Bible, Copyright © 1954, 1958, 1962,
1964, 1965, 1987 by The Lockman Foundation. Used by permission. Scripture
quotations from The Message. Copyright © by Eugene H. Peterson 1993, 1994,
1995, 1996, 2000, 2001, 2002. Used by permission of NavPress Publishing Group.
Scripture quotations marked KJV are taken from the Holy Bible, King James
Version, which is in the public domain.

ISBN
978-1-5255-0917-9 (Hardcover)
978-1-5255-0918-6 (Paperback)
978-1-5255-0919-3 (eBook)

1. BIOGRAPHY & AUTOBIOGRAPHY, PERSONAL MEMOIRS

Distributed to the trade by The Ingram Book Company

Table of Contents

Foreword

Journey—the act of traveling from one place to another, while passing through time, just as Diogenes with his lantern journeyed to find "one honest man," and Mary and Joseph traveled to Bethlehem to bring forth the "Son of God, the Word Incarnate, the Light of the World," so has Carol journeyed by introspection and writing to find her own best self. She has been successful, and I thank her for inviting me to accompany her on this journey.

Joyce M. Gallagher

Dedication

This book is written for and dedicated to my five children, seventeen grandchildren, and Kai Samuel ... soon to be my first great grandson. Also included in this dedication is my mentor, teacher extraordinaire, friend, and sister in Christ, Joyce Gallagher. Without her hours of kind and loving teaching, correcting, listening, and editing, and the technical help of my brilliant grandson, Collin Bartley, this book would never have happened.

Dear Reader,

It seems like such a long time since I embarked on this journalistic adventure. I am delighted that you have chosen to read "My Story." It is my unique tale of life—a life well lived with its good and bad parts, just like yours.

This may be my unique story, but you have one too. As you read about my life, I pray it will inspire you to examine your own story for signs of God's amazing grace.

My desire is to share my life walk with my children from my perspective. Even though we have walked most of it together, I am aware that you can walk and live in close proximity to one another and be totally oblivious to each other's thoughts and feelings about the same events. It has been my desire in this adventure to express my story from my point of view. I am sure there will be points of contention and differences of opinion. It is not necessary to agree with each part, but please accept that it is my story from my perspective.

I have chosen *He Giveth More Grace*, taken from a beloved hymn (Annie J. Flint, 1862- 1932), as the title. I love this old hymn, which is full of the truth of God's never failing and never ending love, grace, and strength given to each of His children as they have need.

The words of the hymn are as follows:

He giveth more grace when the burdens grow greater;

He sendeth more strength when the labors increase;
To added affliction He addeth His mercy;
To multiplied trials, His multiplied peace.

When we have exhausted our store of endurance;
When our strength has failed ere the day is half done;
When we reach the end of our hoarded resources;
Our Father's full giving is only begun.

His love has no limit; His grace has no measure;
His power has no boundary known unto men;
For out of His infinite riches in Jesus,
He giveth and giveth and giveth again.

These words became precious to me as I walked my journey, so in need of each supply. I am praying that you too, dear reader, will find more grace for you journey and that you will prayerfully examine your story for signs that He has been more faithful than you ever thought. For my children, I pray that you will look into the mirror of the Word (not the window) and see yourself as He sees you, and that you choose to allow Him to make you over into His image.

Love and prayers always,

Carol/Mom

Great Grandparents: Generation One

5 You shall not worship them nor serve them; for I, the Lord your God, am a jealous (impassioned) God [demanding what is rightfully and uniquely mine], visiting (avenging) the iniquity (sin, guilt) of the fathers on the children [that is, calling the children to account for the sins of their fathers], to the third and fourth generations of those who hate Me, 6 but showing graciousness and steadfast lovingkindness to thousands [of generations] of those who love Me and keep My commandments.(Exodus 20:5-6, AMP)

I think it's important to glance into the archives of my life and gain some understanding of the ideas and dreams that enabled my forefathers to come to this country, settle, and begin a life of hard work, strong faith, and a deep commitment to make their dreams a reality. From what I have been able to glean, they were a strong, courageous, faith-filled group of stalwarts.

I have a dear friend who tells me that I am a stoic. In case you are unfamiliar with that term, here is Mr. Google's definition: "a person who can endure pain or hardship without showing their feelings or complaining". I fit that definition; however, in my defense, I believe that I come by it naturally.

My dear brother in law, Dr. Jonathan Grothe, has, in his retirement, spent long hours and days collecting data on the Meyer/Menzel family history, which has been an asset to this narrative. Both the Meyers and Menzels came from Germany ... slightly different areas, but they were basically of German descent.

When I first began to write my story, I googled "German discipline." I discovered an article in a 1945 edition of *Parents Magazine* entitled, "How Not to Raise Your Children." It was a tragic picture of childhood in Germany that presents sober lessons for American parents. I have included this bit of information because I think it is of some value in introducing you to my grandparents—your great grandparents. I believe you will find that they fit well into the mode of German discipline.

To bring my grandparents into the picture, I would like to list some adjectives that I feel are descriptive of each. This is how I remember them.

On the Meyer side:

Grandma Olivia Deinzer Meyer		Grandpa Julius Meyer	
Sober	Kind		Strong
Hospitable		Smoker	Hard Work
Stiff	Clean	Artistic	Bread Winner
Enabled	Orderly	Subservient	Giver
In Charge	Religious	Stealthy	Religious
Guarded	Non-nurturing		Quiet

Grandma Menzel Wilhelmina (Minnie)		Grandpa Fred Menzel	
Sober	Sweet	Strong	Hard Worker
Anxious	Kind	Smoker	bread winner
Private	Welcoming	Stern	Sober
Self-depreciating	Self-Sacrificing	Crabby	Faithful
Strong			Godly
Enabler (yielding to Uncle Lew's demands)			

My Meyer grandparents were most guarded and very much in tune with the separation of children and adults. Children should be seen and not heard, unless spoken to, loved if they behaved, and shamed if they did not. These grandparents were strong, stoic, strict, and religious.

My Menzel grandparents lived next door during my growing up years, so of course I knew them better—at least my grandmother. My grandpa died when I was around five years old, so my memories of him are limited. Grandma Menzel, who was a gentle, sweet spirit, always welcomed us into her neat and tidy home, even if we weren't so neat and tidy. I really feel that she loved us unconditionally—good or bad, clean or dirty.

Carol I Vogt

Grandparents: Generation Two

One generation passeth away and another generation cometh: but the earth abideth forever. (Ecclesiastes 1:4, KJV)

Now to my dad, Rudy, and my mom, Elsie, and their seven little offspring. From my recollection of stories told, my parents had an arranged marriage. I never really heard anyone say those exact words, but in putting two and two together, I have concluded that it was arranged, even if it was not named as such. At one point in time, both grandfathers worked for the same paper company in Monroe ... I believe it was the River Raisin. They became acquainted and found they had some common ground on which to build their friendship. They were both of German decent, both Lutherans, and both had families—in fact, just the right families. Grandpa Menzel had one unmarried son, and Grandpa Meyer (to make it more exciting) had four unmarried daughters. The plan was that they would get these unmarried children to an event together, an old fashioned box social—the perfect event!

For this event, the ladies would pack a lovely lunch and wrap it in a beautiful box. All the boxes were then placed on a display table, and the gentlemen would bid on the one they desired the most.

Now the match-making would begin! Lest we think these men and women naive or gullible to be led by the nose to a romance, I suspect a little "cheating," by which I mean those who wished their box to be chosen by a certain young man dropped hints as to which box it might be. As it happened (cheating or not), my father bought my mother's box, and thus began their relationship. After being introduced by way of the old fashioned box social, Mom and Dad began dating, which eventually led to marriage.

They settled in Petersburg, Michigan, where Dad's parents resided and where he had already established his mink ranch. They lived in a small, adequate home on the edge of town ... Madison Street, to be specific. Mom got involved in social things and her church, and Dad built up his mink ranch. Before long, Mom became pregnant; however, she lost that first child in a miscarriage. She became pregnant a second time and gave birth to a daughter, Linda Marie, in May of 1939. Linda seemed to have come into the world with order, cleanliness, and control built into her genes. After all, she was the "first born." These characteristics would sometimes serve her well, but at other times be a bane. She was just becoming her own little self when, in December of 1941, along came her loudmouth, outgoing sister, Carol, who just seemed to step all over Linda's order, cleanliness, and control. There was some bad blood between them, because Dad actually bought them boxing gloves to settle their disputes.

As Linda and Carol were getting used to each other, Mom was finding out how difficult life could be handling two small children. All was not well in Dad's world, either. His precious mink got distemper, an awful viral disease that causes seizures and eventually death. (It is believed that this disease is carried by stray cats. At that time, there was no fence around the mink yard, which left it wide open to strange critters, so Dad erected an eight-foot fence with barbed wire at the top. That became a sufficient barrier for cats and small animals. In later years, however, it did not keep out a burglar.) This disease threatened to wipe out the entire herd. He lost many mink, but was able to isolate the healthy mink and disinfect all the equipment and cages. With a great (but not total) loss, he began again.

Mom found herself pregnant again with child number three. In October of 1943, my sister, Lois Ann, joined the family. Lois was a cute and spunky child, who had some of the perfectionist traits of her sister, Linda. Where Linda was more shy, obedient, and reticent, Lois was feisty and determined to stand up for herself and to have her way.

By late 1945, things had settled in the mink yard. Our small house was bursting at the seams with three busy children and number four on the way, so Dad purchased the large home next door, which had been designed to be a hotel with six bedrooms, two and a half baths, a living room, dining room, kitchen, a play room upstairs, and a mud room by the back door.

It was perfect for Mom and Dad, three girls, and a fourth child on the way, which they hoped would be their son and "heir." Ultrasounds were not heard of at that time, so everyone's "scientific ideas" were from books and articles. My parents prayed, read books, and Mom ate lots of grapefruit, as that was supposed to be the "magic potion" that would produce a male child.

Wonder of wonders, in March of 1946, a male child, Paul John, entered the Menzel family. He was a charming little toy for the three girls, who tried to turn him into a girl at every turn. They put him in dresses and put mops on his head. It was a futile effort. Paul was a delightful child, who looked very much like his father. Dad especially thought that he had the "son and heir" that would follow him in the mink business. That dream never materialized. Soon after we moved into the larger house, Dad's parents moved into the Madison Street house along with Uncle Lew.

By now it was time for us to attend school ... at least Linda and I. We attended St. Peter's Lutheran school for our first years.

The combination of "not enough" money and "not enough" students caused the little one-room school to close. We were then enrolled in Summerfield Elementary—Linda in fifth grade, Carol in fourth, and Lois in second. School was an enjoyable place for us to be. We made new friends and reconnected with others from the previous school. We loved learning and experiencing new things. At home, however, things were becoming more stressful.

Mom found herself overwhelmed with all the children and a super busy husband. She spent a lot of time with her friends to ease the stress. Dad just threw himself even more into his work. Adding to this stress was the arrival of my sister, Ruth Lucille, born in February of 1948. It seemed that there were too many people moving in too many directions. Order, peace, and quiet were totally absent from the scene. I really think that Ruth got stuck with the very worst position in our family. She came after the darling, desired son and was squashed between two cute little sisters who needed lots of attention. Dear Ruthie got the short straw.

By now the older girls were working in the mink yard. Some of them loved it, and some of them not so much. I fit nicely in the latter category. I didn't like being out of doors; I didn't like mud on my bare feet or walking in wet grass, and I didn't like the smell of *mink*, or raking their manure. My two sisters fared better than I at this task. No matter how hard I tried, my work never quite passed Dad's inspection.

At some point during these years with Mom's many absences and Dad's detailed attention to his work, Linda became by default the third parent. I believe that Linda, with her clean, neat, perfectionist personality, felt compelled to be "mother" to this unruly gang of siblings. We didn't recognize Linda as an authority figure, and as such did not yield to her control. This proved to be too much for a nine or ten-year-old child who was hospitalized at least once, possibly twice, for stress. I was too young to grasp the family dynamics, but in retrospect, it was a chaotic and stressful time. Mother handled it with blame and shame for us. Dad just worked harder and stayed in the mink yard longer. As at other times, the upheaval settled and we resumed the crazy life that was normalcy for us.

In January of 1952, my sister, Grace Frances, arrived. Exactly one year and two days later, my sister, Helen Marie, came into the world, bringing childbearing for Mom to an end. These two were total opposites—Grace had dark hair and eyes, and Helen had blonde hair and blue eyes. Grace had a strong, choleric personality, and Helen was shy, gentle, and quiet. We older girls became surrogate mothers to them.

He Giveth More Grace

There's Trouble in Petersburg City

He shall call upon Me, and I will answer him.
I will be with him in trouble and honor him.
(Psalm 91:15, KJV)

I need to step back here a moment to reflect. Mom was indeed a mover and a shaker. If there was an event to be had—civic, social, family, or church—she was there and somehow involved. Mom directed plays and musicals, sang in the choir and sometimes directed the choir, helped out with PTA and chaired the LWML of the Monroe district, and almost always hosted the Menzel/Meyer family reunion at our house. Most of this activity was done away from us. She was very good at what she did, but we wished for and needed her to be at home with us keeping order and peace. She was seldom home in person when we arrived home from school, but we met her on the blackboard. There we found instructions to do many chores that most mothers do during the day.

Meanwhile, back at the ranch ... the gang at 617 Rose Road was functioning as best it could. We seldom took vacations as a family, as Dad could never leave the several thousand mink who needed his undivided attention in the hands of anyone but himself. We did occasionally visit our Struck cousins at a lake where they had a cottage. Our cousins, who were good and comfortable swimmers, loved to dunk their country cousins. As a result, I have no desire to be in the water, and I have never learned to swim. That fear still exists.

We visited my Grandma Meyer quite often. Usually on Sunday evenings after the chores were done and the mink put to bed, we would all cram into our Buick Sedan and sing our way to Grandma's house. No seatbelts, no car seats for little ones, and we usually had someone on our lap so we could all fit. It's odd that we often referred to this as Grandma's house and not Grandma and Grandpa's. Grandpa just seemed to be the little man that stayed pretty much in the basement and out of the way.

It was at Grandma's that we first saw TV and first had a taste of Pepsi-Cola. At Christmas, there were always special treats, such as springerlie and nuts and candy that we never found at our house. When we went on weekends, our aunts took us up to their rooms and allowed us to play with their typewriter, do puzzles, draw or color, or dress up in their clothes.

While Grandma and Grandpa had their TV early on, we did not get ours until much later. But we did have a big radio, and Dad listened to boxing matches and *Amos and Andy*. I also remember listening to a program called *Let's Pretend*, which aired on Saturday morning. I also remember trying to look inside at the light, wishing to be able to see the persons I was hearing. TV finally made that happen!

We all somehow functioned in this rather disordered, chaotic atmosphere. We always had food on the table, and clothes on our backs. We always had work to do, sometimes in the mink yard and sometimes in the house. Breakfast was eaten in shifts as we woke. First come first serve. Dinner was taken together at the dining room table, which was not a cheerful place to be. It was most important to sit up straight with no elbows on the table. We, the siblings, picked at each other, threw barbs across the table, or were lectured about not doing well enough in school. I happened to have "thin skin" and was easily hurt. Rather than helping me deal with my feelings, right or wrong, I was told to leave the table and not return until I could smile—which meant to conform. I learned early and well how to "stuff" my feelings, which later led to colitis. Lunch, when we were of school age, was eaten in the school cafeteria, as we purchased lunch there. I worked in the kitchen in junior high to help pay for my lunch. (I can still smell the strong scent of bleach.)

Once we complained about the food in the cafeteria, and my dad, who was on the school board, took action. He announced that he would be at lunch, and he would be the judge of whether this food was indeed nutritious and suitable. He arrived in his "mink coveralls" and ate lunch with us and declared it just fine. Embarrassed and humiliated, we never again complained about school food.

As I stated previously, school was my favorite place to be. I was accepted, chosen, and made to feel as if I had some worth. I enjoyed friends, cheerleading, being a Queen Candidate, band, many dates, serving as a class officer, and being on the student council. I never wanted to feign sickness to stay home. School life was far more accepting and forgiving than my home life. I had lots of friends and lots of dates—many sweet guys who made me feel special—but only one I dated for a long time. I know now that I used him, as he was a great diversion. He cared about me and made me feel special. When he went to college there was a huge gap in my life. I had to wait sometimes weeks for him to come home. Finally, without my "guy narcotic," I ended the relationship.

I had two opportunities my junior year to date teachers. I had no interest in the first; however, at the end of my junior year, the second teacher asked me to stay late on the last day of school and help him clean up the lab. After doing so, he asked if I would like to go over to Dundee and have a root beer, and I consented.

When he took me home, he asked if I would be interested in seeing a movie sometime, to which I replied that he would have to speak with my parents. Surprisingly, they allowed that to happen, telling me subconsciously that dating a teacher was okay. Imagine me catching a professional man who had a job and wore a suit!

In my junior year, I applied to "Youth for Understanding" to be in a choir, under the direction of Lester McCoy, that would tour Europe in the summer 1959. I had taken voice lessons for years and sang often in my community and at school. To my surprise and great delight, I was allowed to "try out" for this choir. As an even greater surprise, I was chosen. Chosen … what a wonderful word! At home, I never really felt chosen. Now I'd been chosen by my teacher, and chosen to be in the choir. I was flying high! That teacher, of course, was your dad. At graduation time, your father asked me to marry him, and I said yes. We had seen some movies, but our dates were mostly on Saturdays, when he'd take me to Ann Arbor for choir practice session.

I must say, that trip was a most wonderful and enlightening one. I was able to taste and smell and see how other cultures lived and conducted their lives. Since we stayed mostly with families, I got a real taste of European life as it was in 1959. My families were very sweet, kind, and helpful. Some of them imprinted on my heart more than others. My very favorite was the Reverend Robert Whyte, who was a Church of England pastor who took a personal interest in me. He gave me his own personal tour of Tunbridge Wells. Pastor Whyte and his wife had two children, Peter and Fiona. Before being overwhelmed with life in general, we corresponded a bit after my return. In one of his notes to me, he wrote that should they ever have another daughter, they would wish her to be me! Can you imagine? I lost contact with him over the years and doubt he is still alive, but I pray God will somehow let him know how much he touched my heart.

After being lauded in every concert venue with stages strewn with fresh flowers, we returned home to the good old USA. Most of the choir went on to college, and me to marriage. That trip opened my eyes to all that was possible—adventure, fun, and learning in a different atmosphere. I can't say that I didn't have second thoughts about both marriage and college, but college was never offered at my house, and neither were adventure and fun!

Back home, off my pedestal and down to reality, the wedding plans began in earnest. Actually, my mother planned it all. In fact, it was her dream wedding. At this point, I just wanted freedom from my family and still thought I was marrying Prince Charming and headed for life in the city, where I could be involved in music, art, or theater. It was just, "Let's get this show on the road!"

Since my parents couldn't allow me to marry a non-Lutheran, your dad obediently took the required classes to become a full-fledged Lutheran. We had our marriage counselling with Rev. H.B.Fehner, who seemed more enamored by my professor/teacher fiancé than our future married life.

Jumping from the Frying Pan into the Fire

But now, this is what the Lord, your Creator
says, O Jacob,
And He who formed you, O Israel,
"Do not fear, for I have redeemed you
[from captivity];
I have called you by name; you are Mine!
2

"When you pass through the waters, I will be
with you;
And through the rivers, they will not over-
whelm you.
When you walk through fire, you will not
be scorched,
Nor will the flame burn you.
3

"For I am the Lord your God,
The Holy One of Israel, your Savior;
I have given Egypt [to the Babylonians] as
your ransom,
Cush (ancient Ethiopia) and Seba [its province]
in exchange for you. . (Isaiah 43:1-3, AMP)

On December 26, 1959, your dad and I officially became Mr. and Mrs. At some point between August, when I returned, and December, Dad announced that he had bought a farm. I wasn't asked nor did I set eyes on the place until the "deed" was done. In my naiveté, I still thought that was fine. The fact that still escaped me was that a farmer's wife worked alongside him on the farm. I seemed to be jumping from the frying pan into the fire, but I was so swept along by all the wedding events that I was not thinking that far into the future.

There was a house on the farm, but it wasn't ready for occupancy, so we rented a room in Petersburg until we could move in. A most undesirable plan! Dad taught all day and then we went to the farm where he installed a new heating system. By March or April, we were able to move in with heat, hot and cold running water, and a table saw in what would be our living room. After school and on weekends, we continued to work on making that place our home. Before the work was complete, I discovered that I was pregnant. In mid-October, Dad was harvesting soy beans and needed someone to drive the truck so he could unload the soy beans into it. Well, I looked around to see who else might be available, but there were only three persons living on this farm—one was operating the combine, and one was in utero, so guess who would drive the truck? Driving across the harvested rows was one bumpy ride. I always wondered if the baby got frustrated with all that jarring motion. I think at that point my dream of music, the arts, and theater had sprung a leak and was slowly losing all its air. Pretty much totally deflated.

Although most farmers headed to their fields early in the morning and stayed until dusk, your father had a full-time teaching job. Dad was an excellent teacher and a very intelligent man ... near the top of his class always. Along with that, he was a very driven man. Work became his drug of choice. It seemed that he lived in a dream world, never really sure what he wanted to be or just where he really wanted to excel, but always driven to try it all. In addition to grain farming, we also raised pigs, chickens, geese, cattle, and mink. After the animal phase passed, we tried new things in farming. We grew tomatoes for the Hunt Catsup Company, then vegetables for fresh market, and eventually erected a greenhouse where we began a greenhouse/nursery operation. Some of these enterprises did well; others, not so much. All of them cost us more to run than our profit. We were always "a day late and a dollar short." One thing is for sure—your dad was not a quitter. His motto was "try again or die trying."

October is harvest time for soy beans—a two-man job—so guess who got to be the second man? You got it ... me! Eight and three quarter months pregnant, I learned to drive a stake truck across the bumpy rows of stubble, wondering how my poor child felt with all the jarring.

On October 19, 1960, you, Jeffrey Lynn, arrived in our world. Since there were only ten months between the wedding and the birth, friends and family were showered out and bank account poor, so no shower, no money of my own, and no fancy clothes for my little bundle. Grandma Menzel went with Dad and bought your first wardrobe. Soon we brought you home, and I was quickly dumped into Parenting 101. Formula didn't set well with your digestive system, so I rocked, walked, and sang a lot, wrapping warm clothes over your tummy to try to ease your pain, and repeating the process over and over again. In time, as your digestive system matured, you outgrew this. I was so grateful. You were indeed a charming little guy, with big brown eyes and a fetching smile.

Before very long, I was pregnant again with Jonathan, who arrived on the scene the fifteenth of February, 1962. You were a much easier baby, partially because I now had a clue how to take care of this crying, wiggling creature. You had blond hair and brown eyes, and as your hair grew, it curled. Grandma Vogt saw

Dad in that, and didn't want me to cut it. I complied for a while, but pretty soon you found it a lovely place to deposit any food you didn't want, or anything else that needed to be wiped off. So I took courage, became the evil barber, and cut off the curls. You grew into a little man in one fell swoop. As is the case with most siblings, Jeff wasn't fond of you, and for a while chose to ignore me and pretend I wasn't around. Eventually, he rejoined the family circle, and life went on as normal for a bit. You boys did everything together. Living in the country with homes far apart, you learned to play together. I became pregnant again in 1963, and my earnest wish for a little girl came true.

Early in 1964, Grandpa Vogt began to have some physical issues. He was eighty years old. Dad spoke with Grandpa and Grandma by phone daily, and by the end of January, we brought them both home to live here so Grandpa could get the medical attention he needed. Grandma Vogt didn't drive, and Grandpa was unable to do so at this time.

Our doctor made a house call and determined that Grandpa needed to be hospitalized. He went to the hospital and lived for one more week before succumbing to multiple organ failure on February 1, 1964. The day after the funeral, Grandma went into a diabetic coma, and I had to call Dad and get him home to help.

Jennifer arrived on March 1, 1964, and Grandma Vogt came to stay with us. Grandma was in the early stages of dementia. She never adjusted, which I can totally understand. She was ripped from her home, lost her dear life-companion, and was now stuck in a home with busy children, a pretty much absent son, and an exhausted daughter-in-law who ended up with a breast abscess that required surgery. I was also trying to finish a college class by extension from Eastern Michigan. Life was not a bowl of cherries, but rather the pits.

My family had always been involved in the local church, and I had always tried to read my Bible. As children, we attended

Sunday School as well. In my church, I heard lots of law and very little grace. Absolutely nothing was working for me now. I well remember throwing myself onto my bed and crying out to God.

"It's really, really black in my life right now," I said to Him. "If You are out there, You need to show yourself, because I cannot find my way out of this dark, and I see no light at the end of this tunnel." I must say that it was the only time I can remember wanting to die! I left that dark place that day no better than when I came to it, except that I had been able to tell God just how I felt. Now it was up to Him.

Within a few weeks of that conversation with God, our pastor at Trinity preached a sermon on eternal security. Toward the end of that sermon, he asked how many in the congregation knew for sure they would go to heaven. I could not raise my hand, and my heart was heavy. He then proceeded to tell us that if we had repented of our sins and received Jesus' atoning sacrifice for our sins, we could know assuredly that we were already citizens of heaven. I cannot adequately express the joy that I felt as I heard those words. There are truths you can hear and know in your head, but they won't set you free until they travel from your head to your heart. It was as if I had just found the missing piece of the puzzle of my life. My heart began to sing. I felt as if all of heaven was singing with me, and I indeed think they were. As I opened my Bible to read, it became alive to me. I began to understand God's great love for me, and His wonderful plan for my life. I knew that this Bible was indeed His instruction book for living for Him. That year for Christmas, my only request was a new Bible. I cherished that gift and still do!

By September of 1964, Grandma Vogt was in bed most of the time. Once again, the doctors came and told us that we could put her in a nursing home; however, she had no will to live, and we chose to care for her at our home.

Now what was I to do with a baby, two toddlers, a very busy husband, and a dying mother-in-law? God brought us an angel … or at least she was that to me. Dad's mother had a dear friend, a widow who lived here, there, and everywhere. When she heard about your grandma, she volunteered to come and stay with us. Auntie Mim was a tall, sweet lady with lovely white hair. She came, she cooked, she baked, and she sat long, lonely hours with your grandma. All of that made it possible for me to do the rest. Grandma died in mid-September, leaving all of you with just one set of grandparents. Back at the farm, life resumed its normalcy, such as it was. We moved all Grandma's furniture that we wished to keep from the house in Trenton and sold the house, ending that chapter in our lives.

He Giveth More Grace

Pick Yourself Up, Dust Yourself Off, and Start All over Again

When we have exhausted our store of endurance,
when our strength is gone ere the day is half done,
when we reach the end of our hoarded resources,
Our Father's full giving has only begun.

We moved from grain crops to vegetables when Dad secured a contract to grow tomatoes for Hunts. That involved building migrant housing and hiring help. The question arose yearly: Would we be offered another contract with Hunts? Eventually, small operators such as us were dropped for larger ones with newer machinery and updated farming procedures. We then moved on to fresh market gardening—tomatoes, cabbage, cauliflower, peppers, and melons (all labor intensive crops).

I am sure that you will remember standing at the grading table late at night, packing tomatoes and loading the truck for market. Dad would sometimes be able to take it to Detroit, sell out, and be home in time to go to school. I am sure you also remember the wake-up call, hearing Dad sharpening the hoes so we could all go off to work. Hi Ho, Hi Ho, it's off to work we go!

By now our fourth child had arrived. Janel Marie was born on June 6 1967. She came kicking and screaming into the world, and with her came the dreaded colic. As before, we rocked and rocked, and I began to see how mothers could lose their tempers, even though a child can't help what's happening. I developed a great empathy for moms with colicky babies, or even fussy babies. Being a mother is not an easy task; in fact, it is really exhausting. As we now found ourselves running out of space, Dad built what we have ever since called "the new room," which was really a larger dining area and living room space.

Finding joy in the Lord and assurance of salvation was wonderful, but old habits die hard and rarely die without major effort. I was a super stuffer. By that I mean that I didn't always deal with the stresses in my life, and I was eventually diagnosed with colitis. If you avoid conflict to keep the peace, you start a war inside yourself. I was given medicine, which only made me sleepy, and with four children, I did not have the luxury of a nap.

About that time, a friend from Bible Clubs said there was a movie playing in Toledo that she thought we should all see. It was *The Cross and the Switchblade*, the true story of David Wilkerson and Niki Cruz, a gang leader. David, following God's word to him, went to New York City to build a church and to minister to the hard-to-reach persons in the gangs. He bravely walked right into their lives and demonstrated and shared his love for Jesus with them. They came to his church, where Niki got saved and filled with the Spirit. We were so awed by this true story that stirred a hunger and thirst for more of God's Holy Spirit. We heard that there were charismatic meetings being held in the Mother House of St Mary in Monroe.

We took courage and marched ourselves straight into those meetings, where we were met with love and compassion and felt the power of God (where we sang and prayed and studied about the Holy Spirit). After a few weeks, we decided to stay afterward and be prayed for to receive the filling of the Spirit. No lights, bells, or whistles, but a still, quiet sense of God's love and peace, and a new language accompanied those prayers. Some of us coming from a Lutheran background were a visited with a few questions. We decided to visit a gathering of Lutherans who were seeking the same experience. Here we found a strong sense of the Holy Spirit. I have never heard angels sing, but when that group of worshiping people began to sing in the Spirit, it was absolutely heavenly. The melodies rose and fell as if being conducted by a holy conductor. Harmonies and chords blended in one heavenly, worshipful praise. We just seemed to float out of that place that evening.

My experience at that time in my life deepened my faith and strengthened my walk with the Lord. It increased my faith and belief that God had made provision for me to walk with Him in holiness. The apostle Peter says in 2 Peter 1:3: *"His divine power has given us everything we need for life and godliness through our knowledge of him who called us by his own glory and goodness,"* (NIV). I wanted to live that holy life. I needed to trust and obey. The colitis was gone, and I never took the medicine. What an awesome God we serve!

Wanted—Peace in the Midst of Chaos

Trust in the Lord with all thine heart; and lean not on thine own understanding. In all thy ways acknowledge Him and He shall direct thy path. (Proverbs 3:5–6, KJV)

Back to the farm. We thought our family was complete; however, God had another plan. In 1973, I became pregnant again, and in January of 1974, Julie Kristine joined our family. She was a delight. You kids were all at a place where you could enjoy her—except for Janel, who wanted us to take her back where we got her. Impossible, of course. Julie had the "wonderful milk" issues that Jeff and Janel experienced as well, but by now there were other choices of formulas, and soy worked. She was our only child with blue eyes and very curly hair. She brought great delight to us. She definitely got the very best spot in our family.

During this period of time, we were exploring a change in churches. Dad wanted to try the Toledo Gospel Tabernacle. It sounded wild to me, but if he would attend with us, I was willing to give it a try. I was awed by what we found there—a wonderful group of loving people who made us feel welcome, a great choir, and a marvelous preacher of the Word. We began attending when Julie was a baby and stayed for almost ten years. For me, the Toledo Gospel Tabernacle (now called First Alliance) was a most wonderful place to grow in my faith. We went on Sunday Morning, Sunday evening, and Wednesday nights as often as we could, even though we lived forty-five minutes away.

Aunt Clara, who had a multitude of emotional and physical issues, came to stay with us in 1978, because she wasn't functioning well in her home. Clara arrived in a somewhat depressed state and brought with her a drawer-full of prescription drugs. Her pattern was to see one doctor until he or she could no longer help, and then move on to another doctor until he or she could no longer help. It seemed to me that doctor one failed to pass on adequate information to doctor two; consequently, she had enough meds to sedate an elephant.

Although living with a depressed person is difficult, we had some fun times as well as very stressful times, but overall the bad days far outweighed the fun days. I was never sure which Clara would emerge from her room in the morning. On bad days, it was gloom and doom, and on good days, doom and gloom were somewhat absent. She loved being with the kids, especially Julie. She attended church and Jeff's football games with us. Mostly she sat and thought and stared blankly out the window. She loved playing euchre and rook with Jon and his friend, Al, who always cheated so they could win.

Being the "pleaser" that I was, I was certain that I could help her with God's Word and prayer; however, she simply seemed unable to believe that God's promises in His Word were meant for her. Having experienced depression to some degree myself, I know that no person or pill can easily bring us out of that deep, dark pit. We need to take the steps necessary to walk out. Clara seemed unwilling, or maybe unable, to take responsibility for her part of the bargain. Depression is a horrible pit to fall into, but with God, nothing is impossible. To quote Corrie Ten-Boom: "No pit is so deep that God is not deeper still."[1]

With a house full of teens, pre-teens, and a four year old, you may wonder why we added this burden to our already overstressed life. Let's just say that there was a debt to pay. Clara stayed for two and a half years. Since we were all being affected by the cloud hanging over our home, we finally said she would have to find another place to live. She went to the Lutheran Home and died at age sixty-two.

We had a great Christmas in 1978, and all seemed well when very soon after Grandma called Grandpa for supper and got no response. Uncle Paul lived close by and went to the mink yard to see what was going on and found him unconscious. He had suffered a major stroke, which later that evening ended his life here on earth. Grandpa's death in early 1979 left Grandma with a dilemma. She had to leave our family home, and she had to get a job and provide for herself. She worked a number of places where room and board were provided. Eventually, she was able to get into Rawson Place in Dundee, a senior housing development. She made new friends and got involved with senior activities and seemed content. However, her children would soon have to face a very large elephant who sat for years in the middle of our lives. This particular elephant had a name—alcoholism. It is not the cute little Dumbo of cartoons, or the Horton of Dr. Seuss. It was a cruel, life-stealing and family destroying monster! We all knew it was present, but until we were forced to, no one confronted it or talked about it.

Grandma was doing dangerous things under the influence. She burned a hole in the carpet of her apartment, nearly ran over several persons with her car in her community, and was blacking out and falling. As a family, my siblings and I were forced to

---

1   Boom, Corrie Ten. *In My Father's House: The Years before the Hiding Place*. Eureka, MT: Lighthouse Trails, 2011. Print.

intervene. She willingly gave up her car, but resisted the hospitalization required for an alcoholic to dry out. Because we were her children, we sat through classes to understand how this had affected each of us and to discover the role that we had played. This was eye opening, to say the least. Grandma was angry with all of us, which was, for me, most difficult. I'd had a very good relationship with her and felt absolutely horrible that we had to face this mess. Left to her own devices, she would either do herself in, or worse, get someone else killed. She could not go back to her apartment without a change. She spent thirty days in the treatment center in Saline, where we were able to visit her after the first couple weeks, but only on a limited basis. Those were hard days for us all. Her accusations made us all feel as though we had deserted the person who'd cared for us all our lives. After the thirty days, she went back to her apartment. She was given a drug called Antabuse, which would make her violently ill if she drank alcohol. Addictions are strong and die hard, and it takes all you have to kick them. I personally do not know how anyone can "kick" an addiction without the power of an almighty God.

Grandma never really accepted that she had a problem, and one sunny day she sat outside, drank a beer, and had a serious stroke. That eventually landed her in the Lutheran Home, where she resided for nine years ... with little or no meaningful communication. Finally, we were called and told that she needed surgery, as it was suspected that she had either cancer or a gall bladder issue. According to the doctor, she could just ignore it and let it take its course, or she could have surgery and possibly resolve the problem. Because it seemed there was a possibility for some measure of health, we chose the surgical route. During surgery, it was discovered that she was full of cancer, which eventually took her life. We took comfort in the fact that even though we were unable to communicate for all those long years, God's power transcended our minds and He was able to speak to us in any situation, even if we were silenced by illness.

With Grandma "finally home" and at peace, we all sought to resume our lives—my siblings to theirs, and we to ours. We were full force into the greenhouse nursery business, which began as a stop-gap measure to insure healthy seedlings for our fresh market items. We had been having trouble getting seedling from the south, so we drove to Georgia to pick the seedlings up, but many were limp and unusable. It was reasoned that if we grew our own, they would be fresh when we were ready to transplant them into the field; however, "my prince" was never satisfied with a small thing. When the cabbage went well, it was decided to do other things, such as tomatoes, peppers, and eventually flowers. I took my little one, Julie, to the greenhouse, and transplanted the seedlings into flats to grow in for sale in early May. The whole process began in December and ended in mid-June.

It was in that lonely place that I began to meditate on scripture. I took my little Gideon New Testament, propped it up so I could read while I worked, and began to grow in my walk with the Lord. I didn't want to grow flowers, and I didn't want to transplant (a tedious boring job), so rather than focus on the gloom and doom of the day, I chose to refresh myself with the Word. I learned many lessons in that place, mostly because I was always at odds with the Lord about my situation, and He always told me the truth that I frequently did not want to hear. I learned that my life wasn't mine... it was His. He had a plan, and the sooner I co-operated with His plan, the sooner I would have peace in my heart.

As time went on and the greenhouse grew to eight houses, we hired more help. Transplanting wasn't as boring, as my co-workers added much to my life. As we grew, we expanded from just selling here at home to the point where Dad began taking the plants to the Detroit Eastern Market. My job was to stay at home and run the business on Saturday while Dad and some of you kids went to

Detroit. That was a really long day—leaving at 2:00 a.m. and not returning until 5:00 or 6:00 p.m.

The Detroit Eastern Market was an interesting place to be. I liked it a lot more when I could just visit and shop and not have to work. As you kids grew and left for marriage or college, Dad needed to hire other workers, which caused an ever-changing scene. Julie was the last to leave home, so she got stuck with a long trek at the market scene, but she enjoyed it. She was her dad's right hand person for several years and a great recruiter of workers from her high school friends. All of you children worked in the greenhouse or at the market during your growing up years. The boys worked in the field with Dad, where you all learned how to work hard and not complain (at least not audibly).

How I Remember Your Beginnings

And he said unto me, "My grace is sufficient for thee: for my strength is made perfect in weakness," (2 Corinthians12:7, KJV)

You grew up one by one, each with your own particular bent. Jeff, being the eldest, likely got the brunt of our parenting inexperience. Jeff was a sweet child, strong and stoic like his mother. We took him everywhere with us. As years pass so quickly, Jeff was soon ready for school. I so remember that big yellow bus coming for you, and you just marched up the steps like a man. No time for tears until it was out of sight. I soon saw that you were a good student and quite neat and particular about yourself and your work.

There were farm jobs for you as soon as you were able. As you became a strong and sturdy young man, Dad would always have new jobs for you to do that kept you busy after school and on weekends. As high school approached, you became interested in sports. You played varsity football, basketball, and baseball. Dad and I enjoyed watching you play. I didn't worry too much about football … I always thought whoever ran up against you would get the worst of it. Basketball was another story. Football has pads and helmets, but basketball has sharp elbows and an unforgiving wooden floor. I remember you getting charley horses during the game and writhing on the floor with that horrible muscle-tightening pain. I so wanted to leave my seat and help, but I knew, of course, that moms don't belong on the football field or the basketball court.

You learned how to work hard at home, but the pay wasn't much … mostly nothing but bed and board. So off you went to KFC, where you learned how the Colonel fried his chicken. Later you worked for our competitor, all so you could have some money of your own and buy your own car, which you did—a bright red charger, if I remember right. It was great not to have to drop you off and pick you up from every practice, but I often wondered just how fast that car went when we weren't looking … probably a very good thing I didn't know, as I might have had some pretty anxious moments. I did assign you guardian angels each day, and a testimony to their protection is that you are still here today.

After graduation and a party put on by you for your friends with beer (which was not used in our house) and with classmates traipsing in and out until the wee hours of the next day, you finally headed off to Lincoln Tech, where you became a diesel mechanic. While at school, you worked for UPS. We came to visit and found an engine in the bathtub and some healthy-looking cockroaches living in your kitchen. After graduation from Lincoln Tech, you got a job with Caterpillar, and I can't remember where else, but as times got tougher, you were laid off and bravely endured long months of unemployment. You continued to play on the civic teams with your old classmates from Ida. To this day, you have not met that "special person" with whom to spend the rest of your life, but that's okay with me. My desire for all of my children is for them to be happy, gainfully employed, and following Jesus … not necessarily in that order. You have a job, a home, and good friends. I am still waiting for the Jesus part.

Shortly after Jeff arrived, Jonathan was born. You were a much easier baby, most likely because I was now an experienced mother. You always had a soft heart, full of vim and vigor, and seemed to think the world was yours to explore. As you began school, I could soon see that you would also be a good student, in spite of being under the tutelage of a rather unusual teacher. You and your pal, Al, somehow survived. This teacher liked to tie misbehaving kids to their chairs or tape their mouths if they talked too much. She also sent me a note with directions on how to hard boil an egg when the one you had in your lunch wasn't quite done. That wouldn't happen in a classroom today. Then there was the fifth grade teacher that you fell in love with. No feigning sickness that year!

During those elementary days when we had migrants, you and Berto decided to see what happens when you throw fuel oil on a wall and light it. The corn crib burned to the ground, and we were shocked to think our little "Ony" could think of such a thing. It must have been that creative, yet mischievous, mind of yours. I do think you learned your lesson, as we had to call the fire department, which created quite a scene. I also remember the red high top tennis shoes that were absolutely needed and would make you run at the speed of light. You put those shoes on and headed down the driveway at what you thought was breakneck speed, expecting at any moment to be airborne. Also, of course, I remember you trying out for basketball as a freshman and what a great disappointment that was. Dad and I took you with us to the U of M versus Purdue football game to ease your grief. You had a nosebleed that lasted almost the whole way there. I think it was a result of the loss you were experiencing. You did play baseball and did well at that. Dad tried to pay you to play football, but you had no part of that.

You were a good student, and when you were approaching graduation, Dad encouraged you to go into teaching. Off you went to MCCC and then to U of T. You too had to get a job to help pay for your car and school. You worked for Friendly's, where you fell into a nasty trap set by Nick Ohlers. He purchased beer and encouraged you to drink with him in your cars after work. You thought, as many over-the-limit drivers do, that you could drive home safely; however, a policeman saw you swerving, so you were arrested and spent the night in jail. A most memorable moment for me. No mother wants to get a call from the county jail telling her that her child has been arrested for drunk driving. I didn't sleep that night. Dad wanted me to wait until he came home from school to get you out, but I said no way and proceeded to do it myself. Thanks to Tom Schultz, who got you off on personal recognizance, you and I had a very quiet ride home. That was a turning point in your life, for which I will be eternally grateful. God used that time to bring you back into fellowship with Him, and you have served Him faithfully ever since.

Eventually, you were hired as a teacher at Dundee High School, and recently retired from there. God brought Karin into our lives, and we couldn't have handpicked a sweeter, kinder, or more suitable mate for you and addition to our family. Together you brought us three beautiful kids who are like their cousins— smart, talented, and living for Jesus. I am blessed beyond measure.

You, Jennifer, came along next. You were the little girl I had wished and prayed for, and you came into much tumult. You were a delight and, thank God, not a fussy baby. In spite of being shifted here and there for various reasons, you were a bubbly, outgoing child. You too thought the world belonged to you and would have gone home with anyone who smiled at you. You held your own with two rough and tumble brothers, and were included in much of the farm/greenhouse work. You have your father's scientific bent.

Due to a mess in our home life and a very unruly school bus, I chose to send you to State Line School. I did that for a couple years and then couldn't handle the cost, and you girls were ready to return to Ida. I am not sure how that affected you, but I did it because I thought I was protecting you from harsh words and nasty kids. You did well at school, enjoying band, flags, and journalism.

Not sure where to go after graduation, you finally chose the navy. After long delays, you were recruited and off you went, while I was sadly out of town. A couple of things I remember about that period were the harsh reality for you of navy life, and being a female in a predominately male environment. You came home with a very sore, abscessed throat, unable to see a civilian doctor, and had to wait for a week before returning to base on a plane with your ear and throat on fire. My heart cried—a mother unable to help her hurting child. However, God kept you safe, and eventually you got the medical care you needed.

After the navy, you went on to become an emergency medical technician, a Monroe City police woman, and a registered nurse—most of that while raising your family. Leon came into our lives as you two began your life together. He has brought us such joy and fun, because he has a way of making life less serious. Four beautiful grands from this union! Again, each one smart, talented, and loving the Lord. How blessed we all are.

You have chosen to home school your children, which I think is admirable, and I believe you have done a good job. However, I believe our relationship has suffered as a result. No time for just you and me, no shopping trips, or time to just eat or talk together. I guess I want it *all* and should know by now that it is not possible.

Three years after Jennifer, you, Janel, arrived in June of 1967. Dad was finishing the school year at Mason. In the fall, he would be leaving Mason for Bedford; we were building an addition on our house, plus we had all the other farm responsibilities. In other words, with the addition of one more colicky baby, I was feeling pretty overwhelmed. I remember rocking you for hours, rarely getting enough sleep with you sleeping only one or two hours at a time. To add insult to injury, you brought back up most of what I fed you. You looked like a waif. You were skinny with very little hair. I had to tape bows on your hair so people would know you were a girl. You did eventually outgrow that difficult stage and became a "regular member" of the family. I can better understand how mothers can get angry with babies when they forget that the baby can't help what's happening to them. It's not a place for the weak. Being a mom is a tough job.

With a better diet and food staying down, you grew into an energetic child. That may be an understatement, as your dad nicknamed you Butterfly, because you were very seldom still. You zipped and flited everywhere, seldom slowing to sit for even a moment. Busy with this and busy with that … never stopping until you fell asleep at your post.

You outgrew that scrawny beginning and became a beautiful young lady. You had a heart three sizes too big. You always cared for the down and outers, bringing all your stray finds home. Most of them turned out to be very nice people, just not the most popular in your class.

Your middle name should have been "creative." You made something out of nothing and continue to do so today—sewing new clothes for Mark out of his dad's old suits to your on-line business and craft shop. I am so thankful to Pastor Bozeman (at Bedford Alliance Church) for loving you back into the kingdom and getting you involved in a youth group. It was there you met Mark. It seemed you two were glued together from the first. Eventually, Mark finished college and got a job … of all places at Twentynine Palms, California—thousands of miles from home.

Against our wishes, you did not finish your last semester of school. We planned a wedding, and off you both went to the desert. We were not certain how all of that would work, but God providentially matured you both and placed you in good churches with godly friends. You became contented desert dwellers. Mark has grown tremendously and has been able to keep you from dragging him into bankruptcy, but also has allowed you to take over the whole house for weeks each year as you plan for your open house where you sell your crafts. Together you have given us four very special grands and two grands-in – law, each with his or her own special gifts and abilities. I praise God for each of you, and for all He has done to keep you and foster you—even in the desert. As of this writing, I await the arrival of my first great grandchild, due in a few months. That must be a mistake … I can't be that old.

We were certain we had our little family—two boys and two girls—perfect and neatly packaged! Then we got a bit of a surprise as along you came, Julie … seven years after Janel. Just when I thought I had everyone in school and would have a little free time, you, Julie Kristine, arrived after Christmas in January of 1974. For the first time, after four babies, I had a baby shower, which was a great blessing, as I had given most of my baby items away. You bounded in at eight pounds and eleven ounces—my biggest baby. You were a delight, partly because I was now an experienced mother, but also because the older children were eager to help take care of you—all except Janel, who found you to be a threat. You took Janel's place as the baby and left her as the fourth child, in no man's land. Eventually, Janel decided that we could keep you and that you were acceptable.

Jeff and Jon found unique ways to play, like tying your cabbage patch doll, named Ardra Ardella, to the ceiling fan and watching her spin around while you screamed. Tape recorders were big electronic items at that time. Jon would take you into his room and coax you to say stupid, mispronounced things, and then play them back. He also taught you to run around the couch with his baseball hat on. Each time around, he would cheer for you. And you just obediently did all that he said. You were the boys' little toy robot, who scared your baby sitters when you would cry hard and pass out for a few seconds. They were sure you were dead, even though I warned them that was what might happen.

You had a couple of imaginary friends. I had to open doors for them and set a place at the table. They were quite active for a year or so, and then mysteriously disappeared. You were in Mrs. Brunt's kindergarten class. When you'd come home, you'd go into your room, gather all your dolls and stuffed animals, and sit them on the bed or on chairs. Each one would then be given a *National Geographic* magazine, and you would instruct them to do exactly as Mrs. Brunt had done that day in class. I knew you would likely grow up to be a teacher of something to someone ... or at the least you would always be a boss. You were a good student, a part of the gifted and talented program.

In high school, you became a cheerleader and were a part of the yearbook staff. You attended Journalism Camp at BGU. After graduation, you attended, like your siblings, MCCC and then U of T, graduating with a degree in education. You got a job at Crossroads church as their children's ministry director, and that's where you met Bill. Life began in earnest for you then. You were married, and Bill was the strong, steadying hand you needed. Together, you have given us six precious grands, each as smart and talented as their cousins and—best of all— loving and serving the Lord Jesus Christ. You, like Jennifer, have chosen to home school your children, and I commend you for that. I believe you have done a remarkable job; however, just like with Jennifer, I have not been able to have the mother/daughter relationship I had hoped for. I feel cheated in that relationship. I pray as your children marry that they will include you in their lives, and that your daughters will become not only daughters but also friends, and that you will have quality time together to develop a relationship as such.

"Lo, children are an heritage of the Lord: and the fruit of the womb is his reward," (Psalm 127:3, KJV).

He Giveth More Grace

Prince Richard from My Perspective

My frame was not hidden from You when I was being formed in secret, intricately and curiously wrought in the depth of the earth. Your eyes saw my unformed substance, and in Your book all the days of my life were written before ever they took shape, when as yet there was none of them. (Psalm 139:15–16, AMP)

I didn't lack for dates as a teenager. Most were sweet, kind, and comfortable to be with. We enjoyed dances and movies and proms. I did have one long-term steady boyfriend, whom I summarily dismissed when he went to college, as I had lost my comfort buddy. My junior year was a very busy one. I tried out for the Michigan Chorale and was accepted. That was a thrill for me—someone who rarely left the small burg of Petersburg would now get to see a whole lot of Europe.

One of my classes that year was Chemistry, a really tough class for my unscientific brain. I received a D or D- in that class, barely eking by, and even that was a kind gift. Prince Richard (I will call him Prince Richard because we all want to find and marry our Prince Charming) was my teacher for that class. He was young compared to the other teachers, handsome, and gifted with a sense of humor that made him charming.

At the end of that year, I was asked to stay and help the prince clean up the lab.

I agreed to do so. When the job was finished, he asked if I would like to go to Dundee with him to get a root beer. I said that I would like that. The combination of my people- pleasing personality and the lack of fatherly affection and acceptance made the choice for me. When he brought me home, he asked if I would like to go to a movie sometime. I told him that he would have to speak to my parents about that.

I was surprised that he wanted to take me to a movie, and an even more shocked when my parents said yes. My view, in retrospect, is that they saw an opportunity to marry off one of their six daughters, leaving them with one less mouth to feed and person to be responsible for. Sorry if that sounds harsh, but that's pretty much how it was.

For dates, we went to an occasional movie, but most of all we took trips to Ann Arbor, where I practiced for two hours with the chorale. I graduated in June of 1959, and the prince asked me to marry him right in the middle of my graduation party, offering me a ring he'd once given to his former girlfriend (clue #1: How important was I to him that he offered a secondhand ring?) We exchanged the ring for one of my own. I went off to Europe and he went back to school to complete his Master's degree.

Our wedding was set for December 26, 1959. I would just be eighteen and he was twenty-seven. On a cold, foggy, and icy night with little snow, we became Mr. and Mrs. We left for Key West, Florida for our honeymoon. When we arrived at our destination motel, it was evening. There was a pool at the motel, but because it was night, it was closed and a "No Swimming" sign was posted. His Highness wanted to swim and wanted me to join him. Me, being a rule follower, said that it wasn't a good idea, since the sign said no swimming. (clue #2: The prince didn't mind breaking the rules if it suited him). After he finished his swim, he returned to the motel and came to our door. Instead of knocking, he scratched at it and made growly noises. I opened it just a hair to see what was out there, and he stuck his hand in the door. I promptly slammed the door on his hand. Not a good time to play a joke with a new bride in a strange place … not very worldly smart.

We arrived back home after a week and stayed in the upstairs of a friend's house. That too proved to be a stressful choice for me. Sometime between August and December of 1959, he bought a farm. I wasn't asked if I wanted to live on a farm, nor did I set eyes on the place until the deed was done. (Clue #3: Obviously my opinion didn't matter. It was not about us, but about him.) After several months of working all day at school and the two of us going to the farm to work on the house to make it livable, we left our upstairs room and moved out to the farm. Prince Charming's crown was beginning to tilt a little, and maybe it even lost one of the precious jewels. Farming was not my cup of tea. I thought I was leaving the mink farm for a different life. Soon I found myself pregnant with our first child, so at eight and three quarter months pregnant, I was driving a truck while he harvested soy beans. Bumping across the rows, jarring me to pieces. I wondered how the child I was carrying felt. (Clue #4: Being pregnant at eight months was no excuse for not carrying my load of work—work I didn't think I had bargained for).

In addition to teaching school and farming, the prince also coached basketball. That meant even longer hours away from us. The school had a phone and so did we, but he never thought it necessary to call when he would be late. We'd sit at the table, waiting night after night, until I fed the kids and saved his meal for whenever he would arrive. (Clue #5: First sign that family and the fairly newly acquired wife are way down the line in importance.)

Clink, Clink! I think I just heard a couple more jewels fall out of the crown.

The farming grew and so did the debt. Two attempted mortgage foreclosures quite early in our marriage tarnished the crown a bit more. Actually, the crown was now beginning to become a rather ugly shade of green. (Lesson for me too late: financial issues should be discussed long before the I do's.) Our family was growing as well, with two boys and then two girls and then our last hurrah Julie. Each year brought more work, more stress, and less responsibility for things that mattered for me, such as house repairs and upkeep, our spiritual life, and family times that were not related to work. (Clue #6: Family life, spiritual life, and social life are cast aside when your spouse has an addiction to work.)

The princely crown had now disintegrated into a green blob with a couple of beady eyes as the prince took on more obligations, more acres, and more projects. Too much work, too little profit … but driven to never say die, and on we went. Eventually the prince's health began to fail, and things that would have slowed or stopped another man caused my prince to leap over the obstacle.

Work increased, maintenance decreased, expenditures grew, profit decreased, and debt rose to a new high—much like an over-inflated balloon, ready to burst. With type 2 diabetes, it seems that almost every organ in the body is affected.

My prince, now turned toady, had already experienced triple by-pass surgery, and consequently was on many medications, some of which required constant monitoring. Soon the macular degeneration showed up and we made many visits to St. Vincent's for treatment. We took a number of trips to the ER for various things. Sometimes they kept him there, and sometimes they sent him home. He was very unstable on his feet and fell often, even with me holding on for dear life. We had many visits for vestibular therapy, as vertigo was plaguing him. With heart by-pass, macular degeneration, arthritis, and diabetes all on the scene, you would think he would consider slowing down. Not my toady prince. He could no longer do the steps, and it had been years since he spent much time actually walking around the greenhouse property. He had his good friend, Putt Putt (our riding lawn mower), and the tractor, which both served as his legs. Mr. Determination was still bound and determined to stay true to his "never say die" motto.

Addictions are enslaving things, and had he slowed down without admitting or acknowledging his illness, it would have only turned the toady prince into a monster. I must say that during those caregiving years, I began to see those beady eyes fade and the green blob began to look like a little shiny crown again. I also began to realize that I was not only his wife, but his student, his child, and, lastly, his mother.

During his last Greenhouse season, he began to succumb to the financial pressure. Finding no way out of the mess his addiction had created, he chose to file for bankruptcy. Because he was unable to drive at this time, I took him to those appointments. Bankruptcy is an awful thing to go through; however, it saved my life from obligations that were not mine.

We, the family, also got together without the prince and with Don and Terri Thompson, who guided us through the discussion about whether or not the prince could go to Detroit Market any longer. (For the unfamiliar, that meant getting up at 2:00 a.m., arriving at market at 3:00 a.m., and not returning home until 5:00 or 6:00 p.m. Not a schedule for heart patients.) It was decided that we would confront the prince and tell him he could no longer go to market.

My oldest son, Jeff, and I took on this uncomfortable task. He was not a happy toad at that point; however, as with my mother, it was a necessary thing to do. He actually had not been out in the greenhouse that whole season, except for planting seeds, so he bossed from his chair in the house. I know that was a most difficult pill to swallow. We did it as gently and kindly as we could. It brought several days of silence. During the days of hospital visits and trips to doctor's appointments to treat the huge diabetic ulcers on his legs, the beady eyes and green colored blob faded even more and the crown reappeared with even a gem or two. Those were very hard days for both of us.

One of the last hospitalizations was to insert a pace maker, hoping to keep his heart in sync. His final hospitalization was in ICU. He spent weeks there. It was there he had dialysis, as his kidneys and liver were failing. This was right in the middle of greenhouse season, so the kids helped out and took plants to market. We sold what we could at home. Everyone co-operated and, somehow, we got it done.

In the midst of that frantic selling time, we got a call from the hospital—he was dying. (It was never said, but I believe that eventually he refused the life sustaining dialysis. He hated it). They had moved him to a private room, and that's where we found him—quiet, sweet, and knowing he was dying. Jennifer and I prayed with him, and his earthly crown died. But he got a new and glorious one in heaven—much more beautiful than any he ever wore on earth.

He Giveth More Grace

Evidences of God's Grace

> Now unto Him who is able to do exceedingly
> abundantly above all we ask or think, accord-
> ing to His power that works in us. (Ephesians
> 3:20, KJV)

"Difficult roads often lead to beautiful destinations," (anonymous).

One winter, locked in at home with a new baby (and the enemy telling me she would not live), no car, little heat, and calves being born out of season, I was soooo discouraged. I cried out to God, reminding Him of His words in John 10:10: "*The thief comes only to steal and kill and destroy; I have come that they may have life, and have it to the full*," (NIV). With tears, and pleading on my knees, I cried out to God, reminding Him that His Word said He had come that we might have and enjoy life and have it in abundance.

"God," I prayed, "I am not experiencing the joy or abundance that your Word says I should have." I suddenly envisioned an arm, clothed in a robe with a hand extended and holding a screaming, kicking baby. The Lord spoke to me clearly and tenderly: "My dear child, if you will stop kicking and screaming, I will draw you to myself, hold you, and comfort you". And so He did.

Living on the farm with animals always kept us on our guard. One day with Dick at school, and me six months pregnant, I observed out my window a congregation of our steers enjoying my lawn. I tried to contact Dick at school, but I was unable to talk to him until his break. I was concerned they would destroy someone's property or fall in a ditch and break a leg. I asked to Lord to put His angles around them until I could get hold of Dick. I went about my work, and about an hour later, I looked out to see where they were. Not able to see any in my yard, I headed out my back door to find them. As I passed under the house garage, I saw that they had all gathered there. I closed the door and thanked the Lord for answered prayer and a cow congregation meeting!

Because buying clothing was not at the top of the boss's budget, we went to garage sales, and I was able to buy used clothing from friends with children just a little older. Sometimes people just gave us boxes of clothes. Once we got a box of clothing from an older person. There wasn't much that we could use, but we had such fun trying on girdles, hot pants, and undergarments that were way too big and totally outdated. When you are unable to buy the name brand clothing that your teenagers desire, it breaks your heart. It didn't meet our need for clothes, but we laughed until our sides hurt, and it provided the relief we needed. It also helped us put our thoughts and desires back into perspective.

After the fact ... way after ... I learned that my boys and a few friends decided to climb the electric relay station close to our home. Someone called the police, and they all scurried into a close-by corn field and escaped. I declare that God sent the angels that I had requested and kept them from harm and spared then the consequences of their foolish behavior. I could go on and on as incidents come to mind, but suffice to say, if we take even a glance over our lives, we will see evidences of His grace and mercy— all totally undeserved. Hallelujah!

Epilogue

Difficult roads often lead to beautiful destinations.

As I look back at my seventy-five year journey with its twists and turns, ups and downs, and wins and losses—many of which have been written about here—I realize how blessed I have been.

Everyone has a story—one begun while we were yet being formed in our mother's womb, with every day of our lives charted before one of them came to be. I was given to parents who were given to parents for whom life was a struggle, a puzzle, and a mystery.

From time immemorial, God has given His Word. For ages it has been passed on, originally on papyrus sheets by holy men of God who spoke as God moved on them to do, thus scripting for us the Old and New Testaments as a record of truth and a book of instruction for living a holy life. A book alive with truth that is able to "save" to the uttermost.

My grandparents were men and women of faith to some degree or other. They faithfully attended church. I am quite sure that the depth of faith differed for each one. Most of them depended on their pastor to exposit the word to them and for them. They were not always encouraged to read the Word for themselves. It seemed to me in my church growing up that I heard about God, Jesus, and salvation, but I do not remember anyone seeking to help me learn how to live out the words I heard. I found a measure of peace and comfort in hearing God's Word, but there were lots of rules to follow and not much relationship. When I jumped from the frying pan of home life to the fire of marriage, my faith suffered, as I had no instruction on how to deal with rampant and runaway emotions, fears, and doubts. But as I clung on for dear life, God knew my need and my heart, and He took me through stormy waters and rough seas. Eventually, God brought me new friends who invited me to their Bible study, which proved to be life- giving to me. God brought a pastor to our church who clearly expounded God's Word, and my eyes were opened to His love and provision and my home in heaven in a way I had never understood before. As my eyes were opened and a veil lifted, my relationship with Jesus became a personal and loving one.

As life took its twists and turns, I learned to rely on this loving Savior and found Him truly faithful and patient with my stubborn heart. His Word instructed me that He had promised never to leave or forsake me, and all His promises are true. He, unlike some persons in my life, would never go back on a promise, even if some of them are conditional on conditions being met. The Christian life is a journey, and it doesn't end until our life here on earth ends. We are ever learning and ever growing more and more like our Savior. Ins and outs, ups and downs, bumps and bruises, as well as shouts for joy and great victories are all a part of our Christian walk.

Once it was settled in my heart that I was His and thus a citizen of heaven even now, I began in earnest my walk with my Savior. Between diapers, laundry, meals, and other responsibilities, I determined early on that I would have to take this relationship seriously. I would need to somehow carve out time to spend at His feet, learning all I needed to know.

Being a morning person, I chose to get up early and have that time alone with Him and His Word before the rest of my family was up for the day. For many years, 4:00 a.m. was my special time. If I had to miss it because of sickness or some other reason, I'd lock myself in the upstairs bathroom, turn on a fan for noise, and ignore little fingers and notes shoved under the door. That for me has become a lifetime habit, one I have never regretted establishing in my life.

Getting to know Jesus in a personal way was paramount to my faith walk. He was there for me when the kids were sick, when work was overwhelming, when I felt alone and abandoned, when our debts increased and our profits waned, and when life was just plain hard, never leaving me alone, even though at times I was tempted to doubt. We were never promised an escape from difficulties, but are told to hold on tight and walk bravely through. That I did with varying degrees of faith.

As I began to recognize and understand the generational issues from my past, I chose to be the one person in my family who would draw a line in the sand and declare that "generational sin ends here." As each issue was made know to me, I went to the Word to seek God's solution. I stood on the truth stated in 2 Peter 1:4: *"Everything that goes into a life of pleasing God has been miraculously given to us by getting to know, personally and intimately the One who invited us to God,"* (MSG). Did I conquer all? Am I perfect? It really isn't necessary for me to ask those questions, because anyone who knows me knows that perfect is not the adjective they would use to describe me, or really any human being. I can say that I more quickly recognize these issues as they arise, and they no longer debilitate me.

It was with great joy and thanksgiving that I watched you each grow from childhood to adult. Even with our many trials we stayed together and loved each other. I prayed often for each of you to grow into godly men and women, and God has answered that prayer as well as bringing godly mates into your lives. I am so pleased that we have made a choice to meet once a month as a family. That has bound us together in a crazy, mixed up world. We are instructed in Genesis to be fruitful and multiply, and we have certainly obeyed that word: five children, seventeen grandchildren, and a great grandson yet being formed in his mother's womb.

What a mighty God we serve!

CPSIA information can be obtained
at www.ICGtesting.com
Printed in the USA
LVOW12s0518170717
541524LV00001B/1/P